NAMES OF SOLDIERS

OF THE

AMERICAN REVOLUTION

[FROM MAINE]

Who Applied for State Bounty under Resolves of March 17, 1835, March 24, 1836, and March 20, 1836, as Appears of Record in Land Office.

Published by order of the Governor and Executive Council.

COMPILED BY CHARLES J. HOUSE.

CLEARFIELD

Originally Published
Augusta, 1893

Reprinted
Genealogical Publishing Company
Baltimore, 1967

Library of Congress Catalog Card Number 67-28605

Reprinted for
Clearfield Company, Inc. by
Genealogical Publishing Co., Inc.
Baltimore, Maryland
1996

International Standard Book Number: 0-8063-0184-8

Made in the United States of America

PREFACE.

A hundred and ten years have rolled by since the reverberation of the last gun of the Revolution died away at Yorktown. More than three generations have come and gone, and still our interest increases rather than diminishes in those old heroes who, through long suffering and heroic deeds, achieved our national independence and laid the foundation of the grandest nation on earth. Every scrap of personal history and every tradition of that stormy period is eagerly sought for by the present and rising generations. Societies of the sons and daughters of the American Revolution have been formed, who are doing a grand work in gathering the scattered fragments of personal Revolutionary history and putting them in permanent form, to be handed down to future generations. In that great struggle Maine, though an unknown land and without a name, bore no insignificant part. Her villages were small and her homes scattered, yet from every hamlet and hillside her sons came nobly to the work both on land and sea. It was on her waters that the first naval fight occurred, and through her forests marched one of the most daring expeditions of the war. We are told that when General Washington, with uncovered head exclaimed "God bless the Massachusetts line," he was talking to a division composed of Maine soldiers, citizens of York and Cumberland counties. And now the State has very properly come forward to assist in preserving the record of her honored sons. The undersigned has been employed to compile the record herewith presented from the files of papers in the archives of the State, and it is sent out with the hope that it may assist many in tracing their descent from the patriots herein found.

The resolve of Massachusetts granting land, or money in lieu thereof, also all the resolves of Maine relating to the matter, except a few special personal resolves, have been carefully copied and arranged in the introduction which will be of value to the student of history.

CHARLES J. HOUSE.

Augusta, Me., October 19, 1893.

INTRODUCTION.

Nineteen years before the separation of Maine from Massachusetts, on March 5, 1801, with the view of compensating, in some small degree, her Revolutionary soldiers, the General Court of the Commonwealth passed the following resolve:

COMMONWEALTH OF MASSACHUSETTS.
MARCH 5, 1801.

Whereas, Application has been made to this Court by a number of persons who served in the late American army during the war with Great Britain, praying for a grant of some of the unappropriated lands in this Commonwealth, and as such a grant will promote the settlement of such land, as well as be some reward to those citizens whose meritorious services in the field so essentially contributed to establish our independence; therefore,

Resolved, That there be, and hereby is granted to each noncommissioned officer and soldier who enlisted into the late American army to serve during the war with Great Britain, and who was returned as a part of this State's quota of said army, and who did actually serve in said army the full term of three years, and who was honorably discharged, and unto the children if any there be, if not, to the widow of such noncommissioned officer and soldier, and to them only who enlisted as aforesaid and died in said service, two hundred acres to be laid out at the expense of the Commonwealth, as soon as there shall appear a number sufficient to take a quantity of land that shall be equal to one township of six miles square, to be divided and appropriated under such regulations as the General Court shall hereafter prescribe, within the following limits, viz.: Beginning at the northeast corner of the land now appropriated by the committee for the sale of eastern lands on the eastern line of this Commonwealth, thence running west six miles, thence northerly in a line parallel with the said eastern boundary line, until a tract shall be completed sufficient for each non-commissioned officer and private soldier, their children or widows, as aforesaid to have the aforesaid quantity of two hundred acres or twenty dollars as an equivalent for the aforesaid two hundred acres, to be paid out of the treasury to the selectmen of the town where any such non-commissioned officer or soldier, their children or widows as aforesaid resides, for his or their use and benefit.

And be it further *Resolved*, That where any such non-commissioned officer or soldier has deceased, or shall decease, before he shall get possession of the land hereby granted to him, his children or widow as aforesaid shall be entitled to the same, and in order to secure to the said non-commissioned officers and privates, their children and widows as aforesaid the benefits of this grant,

It is further *Resolved*, That all deeds, mortgages, or conveyances of or bonds or contracts of every description concerning any of said lands which may be made by any such non-commissioned officer or private, his children or widow, before the same shall be laid out and have a settlement made thereon and five acres thereof shall have been brought under improvement, shall be null and void; provided always, that no such non-commissioned officer or soldier, his children or widow shall have any benefit from this resolve who shall not make application therefor within three years from the time of passing this resolve, and who shall not make the aforesaid settlement and cultivation within the term of six years.

And the secretary is directed to publish this resolve in such of the newspapers printed in this Commonwealth as his Excellency the Governor may direct, six weeks successively directly after passing the same.

But it seems that a large number of soldiers living in the then District of Maine did not avail themselves of this law, and fifteen years after the separation the Legislature of Maine passed the following Resolves:

Resolve in favor of certain officers and soldiers of the Revolutionary War, and the widows of the deceased officers and soldiers.
Approved March 17, 1835.

Resolved, That each non-commissioned officer and soldier of the Revolutionary Army, who enlisted to serve during the war, or for a term not less than three years, and actually served not less than three years in said Army—who at the time of his enlistment was an inhabitant of Massachusetts Proper or the District of Maine and is now an inhabitant of this State—and who has not already received a grant of land or money in lieu thereof from the Commonwealth of Massachusetts and each widow of such officer or soldier who at the time of his decease was an inhabitant of this State—shall be entitled to receive two hundred acres of land to be selected from either of the following Townships, to wit: Township numbered two, Indian Purchase, in the County of Penobscot, reserving all the pine timber thereon, the same having been heretofore sold—and letter D, in the second range of Townships west of the east line of the State, in the County of Washington—and each non-commissioned officer and soldier who was honorably discharged before the expiration of three years from the time of his entering the service, in consequence of wounds received in the service, or other bodily infirmity—and each widow of such officer or soldier, and the widow of every non-commissioned officer or soldier who died in the service within three years from the time of his entering the same—shall, if in all other respects coming within the provisions of this Resolve, be entitled to receive a like grant of land to be selected as aforesaid.

Resolved, That the Land Agent is hereby authorized and directed to cause the said Townships as soon as may be to be surveyed and laid out into convenient lots of two hundred acres each; and to execute a conveyance of one lot to every officer, soldier and widow aforesaid, who shall prove his or her claims to the satisfaction of the said Land Agent on or before the fourth day of March in the year of our Lord one thousand eight hundred and thirty-eight. And every such officer, soldier or widow who shall establish his or her claim as aforesaid, before the survey of said land shall be completed, shall be entitled to receive from the Land Agent a certificate stating that he or she is entitled to two hundred acres of land under the provisions of this Resolve; which certificate shall be conclusive evidence to entitle the lawful holder thereof to a conveyance in fee simple, of one of the two hundred acre lots aforesaid, whenever said land shall be surveyed and laid out as herein provided.

Resolved, That the Land Agent is hereby authorized to procure at the expense of the State, from the Land Agent and Secretary of the Commonwealth of Massachusetts, and from the Pension Office at Washington, certified copies of all such documents and records as he may deem necessary or useful in carrying into effect the provisions of this Resolve. And it shall be his duty to keep correct plans of all surveys which shall be made as aforesaid, and to mark upon each lot the name of the person who shall first make choice of the same, and also to keep a record of the names and places of abode and such other material circumstances relating to the several claimants as may be deemed necessary to obviate all disputes respecting the justice of their claims.

Resolved, That every officer, soldier and widow aforesaid, who shall become the owner of land under the provisions of these Resolves, shall hold the same exempt from attachment on mesne process or execution.

A Resolve additional to a Resolve in favor of certain officers and soldiers of the Revolutionary War, and the widows of the deceased officers and soldiers approved March 17, 1835.

Approved February 8, 1836.

Resolved, That whenever any officer or soldier or any widow of such deceased officer or soldier, entitled to the provisions of the Resolve to which this is in addition, shall have died or shall die after presenting his or her claim for military lands, the heirs of such officer, soldier or widow shall be entitled to the same lands in the same manner and proportions as if said officer, soldier or widow had died after his or her title had been perfected under said resolve to which this is in addition—Provided such heirs shall produce a certificate from the Judge of Probate of the County where the deceased last dwelt, certifying the number and names of such heirs and in what degrees—and provided also that whenever the oath or oaths of the officer, soldier or widow was required to perfect his or her claim, such other evidence may be substituted by the heirs as the Land Agent, with the approbation of the Governor shall prescribe.

Resolve additional to a Resolve in favor of certain Officers and Soldiers of the Revolutionary War, and the Widows of deceased Officers and Soldiers.

Approved March 23, 1838.

Resolved, That the Resolve in favor of certain Officers and Soldiers of the Revolutionary War and the Widows of deceased Officers approved March seventeenth, eighteen hundred and thirty-five shall be so construed and carried into operation as to extend the benefits of the same as well to each non-commissioned officer and soldier and to the widow of each non-commissioned officer and soldier who enlisted and served in the army of the Revolution during the war in the line or lines of any other State as in the Massachusetts line—Provided, said non-commissioned officers or soldiers or the widows of said non-commissioned officers or soldiers have not already received a grant of land or money in lieu thereof from any other State; and provided further that said non-commissioned officer or soldier, or the widow of said non-commissioned officer or soldier was an inhabitant of this State on the seventeenth day of March, eighteen hundred and thirty-five, and that the full benefit of said Resolve shall be extended to them in the same manner and upon the same conditions as the said Resolve has been extended to the non-commissioned officers and soldiers of the Massachusetts line.

Resolved, That so much of the Resolve above named as relates to the term of enlistment and service shall be so construed as to entitle to the benefits of said Resolve those non-commissioned officers and soldiers and the widows of such non-commissioned officers and soldiers who actually served three years, although they may not have enlisted for that term.

Resolved, That these Resolves and the Resolves to which these are additional shall be and remain in force for the period of two years after these Resolves shall have been approved by the Governor.

Under these Resolves there were over 800 applications made for land. Many of them could not prove a three years' service; in fact there were many who enlisted late in the war for three years and were discharged on account of the close of the war. To meet these deserving cases the following additional Resolve was passed:

Resolve additional to a Resolve, passed March seventeenth in the year of our Lord one thousand eight hundred and thirty-five, entitled, "Resolve in favor of certain Officers and Soldiers of the Revolutionary War, and the Widows of the deceased Officers and Soldiers."

Approved March 24, 1836.

Resolved, That there be paid from the Treasury of this State, out of any money in the Treasury not otherwise appropriated to each non-commissioned Officer and Soldier of the Massachusetts line of the Revolutionary Army, who enlisted to serve for the term of three years, or for during the war, and was honorably discharged; and to each Widow of such deceased Officer and Soldier; and to each Widow of such of said Officers and Soldiers as may hereafter decease before establishing a claim to the benefits of this Resolve, the sum of Fifty Dollars. *Provided, however*, that in all cases such Officers, Soldiers and Widows shall in all other respects come within the provisions of the Resolve to which this is additional; *and Provided also* that the provisions of this Resolve shall not extend to those who have received land, or may hereafter establish their claim to land under the provisions of said Resolve.

Under this last named resolve there were over 300 applications made for the $50, the larger part of whom had already made application for land and been rejected. There was more or less special legislation under all these resolves, but only two names appear therein which are not found on the files of the Land Office, viz.:

February 24, 1838, Levi Chadbourn of Parsonsfield was granted $50.

March 8, 1838, W. Thomes was granted $50.

These two soldiers probably made application to the Land Office, and had their papers taken off the files to go before a legislative committee. There is no book record to be found of the applicants for money, and several numbered papers are missing.

Thus far no grants of land or money had been made by our State to the commissioned officers, and in 1838 the following resolves were passed:

Resolves in favor of certain commissioned officers, and others, of the Revolutionary War, and the Widows of such persons.
Approved March 20, 1838.

Resolved, That each commissioned officer of the Revolutionary army, who actually served not less than three years in said army, and who, at the commencement of such service, was an inhabitant of Massachusetts Proper, or of the District of Maine, and is now an inhabitant of this State, and who has not already received a grant of land, or money in lieu thereof, from the Commonwealth of Massachusetts, and each widow of such officer, who, at the time of his decease, was an inhabitant of this State, shall be entitled to receive six hundred acres of land to be selected from Letter E in the second Range of Townships, West of the East Line of the State, in the County of Washington.—And each Officer, who was honorably discharged before the expiration of three years from the time of his entering the service in consequence of wounds received in the service, or other bodily infirmity, and each widow of such officer, and the widow of each officer who died in the service within three years from the time of his entering in the same, shall, if in all other respects coming within the provisions of this Resolve, be entitled to receive a like grant of land to be selected as aforesaid.

Resolved, That the Land Agent is hereby authorized and directed to cause the said Township, as soon as may be, to be surveyed and laid out into convenient lots of six hundred acres each; and to execute a conveyance of one lot to every officer and widow aforesaid, who shall prove his or her claim to the satisfaction of the Land Agent, on or before the fourth day of March, in the year of our Lord one thousand eight hundred and forty. And every such officer, or widow, who shall establish his or her claim as aforesaid, before the survey of the land shall be completed, shall be entitled to receive from the Land Agent a certificate stating that he or she is entitled to six hundred acres of land under the provisions of these Resolves: which certificate shall be conclusive evidence to entitle the lawful holder thereof to a conveyance in fee simple of one of the six hundred acre lots aforesaid, whenever said land shall be surveyed and laid out as herein provided. And it shall be the duty of the Land Agent to number said lots, to be surveyed and laid out as aforesaid, from number one upwards, and place the numbers in a box to be kept for that purpose, and each person, who shall be entitled to a lot under the provisions of these Resolves shall, in person or by agent, draw one number therefrom, which shall represent the lot to which such person may be entitled.

Resolved, That the Land Agent is hereby authorized to procure, at the expense of the State, from the Land Agent and Secretary of the Commonwealth of Massachusetts, and from the Pension Office at Washington, such evidence as he may deem necessary or useful in carrying into effect the provisions of these Resolves. And it shall be his duty to keep correct plans of all surveys, which shall be made as aforesaid, and to mark upon each lot the name of the person who shall draw the same, and also to keep a record of the names and places of abode of, and such other material circumstances relating to the several claimants, as may be deemed necessary to obviate all disputes respecting the justice of their claims.

Resolved, That every officer and widow, who shall become the owner of land under the provisions of these Resolves, shall hold the same exempt from attachment on mesne process or execution.

Thirty-three commissioned officers or widows of officers made application for the 600 acres of land. In the following list, which contains the names of the applicants under all these Resolves, the alleged rank of each commissioned officer is given.

After eliminating all duplicates there are found to have been 978 applicants for land or money; or 980 including Chadbourn and Thomes before referred to; of whom 480 were soldiers, and 500, widows.

When the soldier was living, his name and residence are given, followed by his place of residence at the time of his enlistment; but where the widow made the application, the name of the soldier, his residence at the time of his enlistment, place and date of his death, Christian name and residence of the widow are given, followed by the name of her second husband if she had remarried.

The following abbreviations have been used, viz: e indicates place of residence at time of enlistment; d, died; w, widow and m, married.

The name of a town following the name of a soldier or widow indicates their residence at the time the application was made.

In locating persons, as far as relates to the State of Maine, the present name of the town is used when it can be identified, but in some cases this is impossible. Falmouth as the place of residence at the time of enlistment may mean Portland, Falmouth, Westbrook, or Deering, and so Pownalboro covers Alna, Dresden, Perkins and Wiscasset.

With but few exceptions there are papers on file at the State House, giving information in regard to the service of these Revolutionary soldiers, consisting of the declaration of the applicant with affidavits to prove their claim for State land or money and in many cases full copies of papers filed at Washington in their pension claims.

These papers contain a rich store not only of personal, but of war, history; detached statements and broken fragments to be sure, but none the less interesting and real. They tell us in the words of the very actors in that war, of Concord, Lexington and Bunker Hill; of the siege of Boston, of Ticonderoga and Crown Point; of Long Island, Stony Point and White Plains; of the retreat across New Jersey, of Trenton and of Valley Forge; of the surrender of Burgoyne and Cornwallis; of raids into the Indian country, of the cruise of Paul Jones; of the campaign of Arnold through the wilderness of Maine; of camp fare and of prison life.

This compilation has been made with a great deal of care, yet no doubt some errors exist, as it is not always easy to decide between conflicting statements, many of which were made long years after the war, and when the persons making them were very old.

ALPHABETICAL LIST OF NAMES.

Abbot, John, e Woolwich, d Boothbay April 16, 1825, w Rachel, Bath.
Abbot, John, North Berwick, e South Berwick.
Accrow, Silas, e Plymouth, Mass., d Portland about 1816, w Sarah, Portland.
Adams, Jedediah, e Lincoln county, d Bowdoinham July 17, 1833, w Rebecca, Bowdoinham.
Adams, Joseph, Jay, e Concord, Mass.
Adams, Samuel (surgeon), e Truro, Mass., d Bath March 6, 1819, w Abigail, Bath.
Adams, Samuel, Bowdoin, e Harpswell.
Adams, Solomon, Farmington, e Chelmsford, Mass., d Vienna November 4, 1833, w Hannah, Farmington.
Additon, Thomas, Greene, e Duxbury, Mass.
Adley, Peter, Hallowell, e Soper, N. Y.
Akley, Samuel, Rumford, e Topsham.
Albee, Jonathan, Lexington, e Wiscasset.
Alld, William, e Waterboro, d New Brunswick in 1791, w Hannah, Hollis, m Joseph Clark.
Allen, Amos, Dresden, e Dresden.
Allen, Daniel, Bowdoin, e Topsham.
Allen, Daniel, Winthrop, e Winthrop.
Allen, Ebenezer, Hampden, e Rochester, N. H.
Allen, Hezekiah P., e Dedham, Mass., d Bowdoinham January 31, 1826, w Susannah, Bowdoinham.
Allen, Isaac, Minot, e New Gloucester.
Allen, Jacob, Scarboro, e Portland.
Allen, Job, Pownal, e New Gloucester.
Allen, John, e Portland, d Thomaston February 27, 1832, w Eunice, Thomaston.
Allen, Joseph, Gray, e Falmouth
Allen, William, e Topsham, d China April 3, 1834, w Jane, China.

Allen, Wright, e Cape Elizabeth, d Denmark April 7, 1832, w Ruth, Denmark.
Alley, Ephraim, Boothbay, e Boothbay.
Ames, Samuel, alias Samuel Buck, Norway, e Haverhill, Mass.
Andrews, John, e Raynham, Mass., d Minot February 6, 1829, w Betsey, Minot.
Andrews, Samuel E, e Hillsborough, N. H., d Lovell January 1, 1822, w Hannah, Lovell.
Arno, John, e Bath, d Leeds March 30, 1831, w Mariam, Leeds.
Arnold, Robert, Starks, e Middlesex County, Mass., or Kittery.
Atherton, Joel, Waterford, e Harvard, Mass.
Atkinson, William, Lewiston, e North Yarmouth.
Austin, Benjamin, e York, d York April 9, 1826, w Abigail, York.
Austin, David, e Berwick, d Dresden March 18, 1833, w Judith, Alna.
Austin, Jonah, e Falmouth, d Windham September 27, 1833, w Sarah, Windham.
Averill, Ezekiel, Wiscasset, e Alna.
Ayer, Benjamin, Winthrop, e Buxton.

Babb, Peter, Buxton, e Scarboro.
Babbidge, Courtney, e Deer Isle, d Vinalhaven October 9, 1834, w Catherine, Vinalhaven.
Bacon, Timothy, Gorham, e Gorham.
*Bailey, Daniel, e Woolwich, d Woolwich March 13, 1817, w Susannah, Woolwich.
Bailey, Hudson, of Portland, e Portland, d at sea, w Sarah, Portland.
Bailey, Israel, e Bridgewater, Mass, d Buckfield May 20, 1830, w Lucy, Minot.
Bailey, John, e Bridgewater, Mass., d Turner July 19, 1833, w Lucy B., Turner.
Bailey, John, e Portland, d Portland August 13, 1822, w Abigail, Vassalboro.
*Bailey, Joshua, e Woolwich, d Woolwich December 24, 1827, w Sarah, Woolwich.
*Bailey, Josiah, e Woolwich, d Woolwich February 5, 1836, w Mary, Woolwich.
Bailey, Prince, Leeds, e Hanover, Mass.
Bailey, Samuel, e Rowley, Mass., d Milford (Sunkhase) May 14, 1830, w Elenor, Lincoln.

---

* Sometimes spelled Bayley.

Baker, Amos, Skowhegan, e New Ipswich, N. H., d Buffalo, N. Y., October 7, 1814, w Elizabeth, China.
Baker, Samuel, e North Yarmouth, d North Yarmouth August 3, 1826, w Mary, North Yarmouth.
Baker, Silas, Freeman, e Marlborough, Mass.
Ball, John, e Whitefield, d Concord September 3, 1823, w Rachel, Concord.
Ballard, Jonathan, e Andover, Mass., d Temple October 31, 1830, w Betty, Temple.
Ballard, Uriah, Fryeburg, e Wilton, N. H.
Bangs, Joshua, e Falmouth, d Auburn April 23, 1823, w Anna, Auburn, m Woodbury.
Barker, Daniel, e Stow, Mass , d Waterford February, 1824, w Rachel, Bethel.
Barker, James, Westbrook, e Stow, Mass.
Barnes, Joseph, e Harpswell, d Lubec May 28, 1838, w Lydia, Lubec.
Barrett, Nathaniel, Fairfield, e Chelmsford, Mass.
Barron, Jonathan, e Mass., d Minot March 21, 1815, w Mehitable, Topsham.
Barrous, Abraham, alias Barnes, e Sanford, d Cornish Oct. 24, 1819, w Margaret, Cornish.
Barrows, Peter, e Attleborough, Mass., d Camden May 12, 1841, w Elizabeth, Camden.
Barstow, Benjamin, e Newcastle, d Nobleboro August 10, 1824, w Susannah, Nobleboro.
Bartlett, Joseph, e Whitefield, d Montville June 2, 1826, w Hannah, Whitefield.
Barton, Ebenezer, e Windham, d Windham April 15, 1785, w Dorothy, Windham.
Barton, John, e Falmouth, d Salem May 10, 1834, w Abigail, Salem.
Bates, Samuel, e Wareham, Mass., d Fairfield October 18, 1817, w Susanna, Fairfield.
Beckler, Daniel, e Waldoboro, d Greenwood March 25, 1830, w Elizabeth, Greenwood.
Bemis, Thaddeus, Fryeburg, e Waltham, Mass.
Benjamin, John, e Needham, Mass., d Whitefield December 2, 1814, w Betsey, Freedom, m John Decker.
Benner, Christopher, Dennysville, e Abington, Mass.
Bennett, Andrew, Troy, e Mt. Desert.
Berry, George, Greene, e Scarboro.
Berry, Joseph, York, e York.

Berry, Nathaniel, Gardiner, e Gardiner.
Berry, Pelatiah, e Scarboro, d Gray December 20, 1827, w Louisa, third wife, Gray.
Berry, Samuel, e Gardiner, d Auburn August 6, 1816, w Ruth, Auburn.
Berry, Timothy, Cornish, e Scarboro.
Bisbee, Elisha, e Pembroke, Mass., d Sumner December 4, 1826, w Chloe, Hartford, m Stetson.
Black, Henry, Kittery, e Kittery.
Black, Josiah, Limington, e Gorham.
Blackington, James, e Rehoboth, Mass., d Thomaston October 25, 1835, w Elizabeth, Thomaston.
Blair, James, Woolwich, e Woolwich.
Blaisdell, Daniel, e Phippsburg, d Phippsburg February 4, 1829, w Phebe, Mexico, m Howard.
Blaisdell, Jonathan, e Brunswick, w Elizabeth, Brunswick, m Coffin.
Blake, Benjamin, Brownfield, e Gorham.
Blake, John (lieutenant), Brewer, e Wrentham, Mass.
Blake, John, e Harpswell, drowned in Harpswell bay July 14, 1806, w Jane, Brunswick.
Blake, John, e Gorham, d Gorham March 26, 1826, w Deborah, Gorham.
Blake, Joseph, Gorham, e Gorham.
Blake, Willing, Warren, e Wrentham, Mass.
Blakely, Pero, e Bridgewater, Mass., d China December 15, 1814, w Dina, China.
Blithen, Increase, Phillips, e Durham.
Boaz, James, Portland, e Plymouth, Mass.
Bogs, Samuel, e Warren, d Warren October 1, 1834, w Susanna, Warren.
Boies, John, of Madison, e N. H., d March 16, 1833, w Mary, Skowhegan.
Bolton, David, e Frankfort, d Augusta February 4, 1828, w Hannah, Augusta.
Bond, Jonas, Dennysville, e Lincoln, Mass.
Booker, Isaiah, e Harpswell, d Canaan February 23, 1823, w Sarah, Bowdoinham.
Boothby, William, e Scarboro, d Limerick September 2, 1828, w Elizabeth, Limerick.
Boston, Thomas, Kennebunkport, e Wells.

Bosworth, Daniel, Dennysville, e Petersham, Mass.
Bowden, Amos, e York, d Castine December 20, 1820, w Lucy, Castine.
Bowden, Theodore, Penobscot, e York.
Bowker, Levi, Machias, e Scituate, Mass.
Bowler, Ralph H., late of Machias (adjutant), e Massachusetts, w Hannah, Brooklyn, N. Y.
Brackett, John, Harrison, e Falmouth.
Bracy, James, York, e York.
Bradford, Peabody, Minot, e Duxbury, Mass.
Bragdon, Aaron, Corinth, e York.
Bragdon, John, Kennebunk, e Berwick.
Bragdon, John, New Gloucester, e Scarboro.
Bragg, Joab, e Vassalboro, d Vassalboro April 9, 1832, w Lydia, Vassalboro.
Bray, Joseph, Anson, e New Gloucester
Bridges, Daniel, York, e York, temporarily in Wolfboro, N. H.
Bridges, Edmund. Castine, e York.
Briggs, Adin, e Stoughton, Mass., d Anson February 26, 1828, w Abigail, Starks, m Seavey.
Briggs, Jesse, e Taunton, Mass., d Paris February 18, 1833, w Naomi, Paris.
Britton, Jonathan. Otisfield, e Pittsfield, Mass.
Brooks, Samuel, e Buxton, d Porter April 14, 1825, w Lucy, Porter.
Brown, Amos, late of Limerick, e Saco, d Cornish December 1, 1829, w Hannah, Limerick.
Brown, Andrew, Litchfield, e Kennebunk.
Brown, David, Boothbay, e Warren.
Brown, Enoch, Sebec, e Arrowsic.
Brown, Jacob, e Waterboro, d Hiram December 1831, w Rhoda, Hiram.
Brown, Jacob, (ensign,) e North Yarmouth, d North Yarmouth February 28, 1813, w Judith, Windham.
Brown, James, Parsonsfield. e Virginia.
Brown, James, e Newcastle, d Palermo May 28, 1827, w Aseneth, Palermo.
Brown, Jesse, e Gorham, d Raymond December 10, 1831, w Elee or Ela, Raymond.
Brown, Moody, Cornish, e Waterboro.
Brown, Samuel, Oxford, e Milford, Mass.

ALPHABETICAL LIST OF NAMES.

Bryant, Daniel, Saco, e Saco.
Buck, Moses, e New Gloucester, d Sumner, August 24, 1826, w Hannah, Sumner
Bumpus, Shubal, Montville, e Wareham, Mass
Burbank, Eleazer, Belgrade, e Scarboro.
Burgess, David, e Wareham, Mass., d Fairfield Oct. 11, 1832, w Sylvia, Fairfield.
Burnham, Joseph, e Kennebunkport, d at sea about 1793, w Susanna, Kennebunkport, m Proctor, then m Dudley Stone.
Burr, Daniel, e Oxford, Mass., d Mercer March 13, 1834, w Susanna, Mercer.
Burrill, Benoni, e Abington, Mass, d Clinton April 8, 1814, w Lydia, Fairfield.
Burrill, Humphrey, Skowhegan, e Abington. Mass.
Burrows, Jonathan, e Lebanon, d Lebanon January 1, 1817, w Elizabeth, Lebanon.
Bussell, Isaac, Columbia, e Bangor.
Butler, Jonathan, e Georgetown, d Turner January 21, 1827, w Dolly, Turner.
Butler, Phineas, Thomaston, e Union.

Campbell, Alexander, e Massachusetts, d Minot February 15, 1827, w Mary, Minot.
Campbell, James, Monmouth, e Boxford, Mass
Carl, John, e Lyman, d Unity October 17, 1832, w Lois, Unity.
Carlton, Ezra, Letter E plantation, e Nottingham, N. H.
Carlton, John, Frankfort, e Thomaston.
Carter, Hubbard, e Warner, N. H., d Fryeburg September 1803, w Abigail, Lovell, m Abraham Andrews.
Carvill, Henry, e Cape Elizabeth, d. Lewiston July 12, 1823, w Mercy, Lewiston.
Cary, Luther, Turner, e Bridgewater, Mass.
Cash, John, Raymond, e Cape Elizabeth.
Chadbourn, Levi, Parsonsfield. (See Introduction, page 10.)
Chadbourn, Silas (quarter master), e Gorham, d Gorham June 13, 1823, w Lucy, Gorham, m Edwards.
Chamberlain, Jeremiah, e Pepperell, Mass., d Nobleboro October 24, 1831, w Sarah, Nobleboro.
Chamberlain, Moses, e Pepperell, Mass., d Moscow December 9, 1833, w Anne, Norridgewock.
Chamberlain, Silas, e Dracut, Mass., d Minot October 30, 1812, w Susanna, Minot.

Chandler, Joel, e Winthrop, d Winthrop April 19, 1794, w Deborah, Winthrop, m Glidden.
Chandler, Moses, e Concord, N. H , d Fryeburg September 10, 1822, w Mary, Fryeburg
Chapman, Nathaniel, e Lunenburg or Ipswich, Mass , d Kingfield January 2, 1819, w Sally, Starks.
Chase, Ezekiel, Sebec, e Hallowell.
Child, Jonas, e Watertown, Mass.; d Hallowell February 14, 1815, w Anna, Hallowell.
Childs, Amos, Vassalboro, e Watertown, Mass.
Chipman, William, Oxford, e New Gloucester.
Choate, Ebenezer, Bridgton, e Ipswich, Mass.
Church, Charles, Phillips, e Pembroke, Mass.
Churchill, Jabesh, Buckfield, e Bridgewater, Mass.
Chute, Josiah, e Windham, d Windham October 3, 1834, w Mary, Windham.
Clark, John, e Wiscasset, d Whitefield November 9, 1810, w Lydia, Whitefield.
Clark, Joseph, Wiscasset, e Alna.
Cleaves, William, Cumberland, e Kennebunk.
Clough, Benjamin, Monmouth, e Winthrop.
Cobb, Roland, Union, e Plympton, Mass.
Coburn, Moses, Newry, e Dunstable, Mass.
Cochran, John, e Newcastle, d Newcastle March 11, 1793, w Agnes, Edgecomb.
Coffin, Nicholas, Lincoln, e Conway, N. H.
Colbrough, Daniel, e Scarboro, d Denmark November 13, 1833, w Elizabeth, Hartford.
Colby, Samuel, Portland, e Bradford, Mass.
Cole, Barnet, Windsor, e Sutton, Mass.
Cole, Eli, e Kittery, d Buxton December 16, 1832, w Olive, Buxton.
Cole, Isaiah, Waldoboro, e Waldoboro.
Cole, John, e Waterville, d Albion January 11, 1824, w Polly, Albion.
Cole, Samuel, Lewiston, e North Yarmouth.
Collins, Benjamin, St. Albans, e Salisbury, Mass.
Collins, Lemuel, Industry, e Cape Ann, Mass.
Colson, David, e Bath, d Thomaston March 17, 1834, w Mary, Bath.
Cone, Elijah, e Connecticut, d Lovell, w Judith, Lovell.

Cone, Samuel, Hampden, e Saybrook, Conn.
Conn, Jonathan, Bethel, e Northboro, Mass.
Cook, Abram, e Lebanon, d in U. S. service July 15, 1813, w Sarah, Lebanon.
Cool, John, Waterville, e Winslow.
Coolidge, Silas, e Weston, Mass., d Trenton May 13, 1834, w Elizabeth, Trenton.
Coombs, Joseph S., d Brunswick April 24, 1835, heirs, Lucy Coombs and Thankful Given.
Coombs, Samuel C., e Lincoln county, d Bowdoinham October 31, 1826, w Rachel, Bowdoinham.
Cornish, John, Brunswick, e Brunswick.
Couch, George, e Dresden, d Hallowell June 1787, w Ann, Readfield, m Constant Norton.
Couch, John, e Hallowell, d Hallowell March 14, 1830, w Jane, Hallowell.
Cousins, Samuel, e Sedgwick, d Sedgwick August 6, 1835, w Pamelia, Sedgwick.
Crane, Abijah, Fayette, e Dedham, Mass.
Crawford, William, Gardiner, e Bath.
Crediford, Abner, e Kennebunkport, d Kennebunkport September, 1793, w Ruth, Kennebunkport.
Cree, Asa, e Massachusetts, d Waterville October 19, 1833, w Love, Canaan.
Creech, Richard, e Sandwich, Mass., d Leeds June 13, 1819, w Elizabeth, Leeds.
Cresey, Benjamin, Falmouth, e Falmouth.
Crockett, Samuel, Cape Elizabeth, e Cape Elizabeth.
Crosby, Charles, e Smithfield, R. I., d Garland December 17, 1835, w Mary, Garland.
Croxford, John, e Cumberland county, d Newburg December 26, 1820, w Wilmot, Newburg.
Cummings, Thomas F. (lieutenant), e Needham, Mass., d Prospect October 24, 1825, w Mary, Cutler, later of Castine.
Cunningham, Samuel, e Jefferson, d Brunswick September, 1803, w Sarah, Newcastle.
Cushman, Andrew, Leeds, e Plympton, Mass.
Cushman, Joshua, e Bridgewater, Mass., d Augusta January 26, 1834, w Lucy, Winslow.

Dain, John, Lisbon, e Cumberland county.
Daisey, John, e North Yarmouth, d Poland 1831, w Mehitable, Poland.
Damans, Abiah, e Abington, Mass., d Charlotte April 9, 1836, w Lucretia, Charlotte.
Danforth, Abner, Litchfield, e Brunswick.
Davenport, Philip, e Hallowell, d Hallowell April, 1820, w Jerusha, Augusta.
Davis, Aaron, Warren, e Wrentham, Mass.
Davis. Allen, Minot, e Gloucester, Mass.
Davis, Benjamin, Belfast, e Gloucester, Mass.
Davis, Elijah, e Gorham, d Gorham October 5, 1783, w Phebe, Bridgton, m Whitney.
Davis, Ezra, e Gardiner, d Pittston September, 1823, w Abigail, Ellsworth.
Davis, John, e New York or New Jersey, d Cutler April 27, 1836, w Eliza, Cutler.
Davis, John, e Scarboro, d St. George May, 1792, w Eunice, Thomaston.
Davis, John, Waterville, e Saco.
Davis, Joshua, Canton, e Gorham.
Davis, Micah, e Middlesex county, Mass., d Fairfield January 7, 1832, w Lydia, Gardiner.
Davis, Nicholas, e Saco, d Hollis January 14, 1832, w Abigail, Hollis.
Davis, Philip, Fayette, e Windham.
Davis, Samuel, Standish, e Gorham.
Davis, William, Eddington, e Maine.
Davis, William, e Long Island, N. Y., d Fairfield November 29, 1836, w Jane, Sidney.
Davis, William, Whitefield, e Berwick.
Davison, Alexander, Edgecomb, e Tewksbury, Mass.
Day, Nathaniel, Lovell, e Fryeburg.
Dean, Ebenezer, Madison, e Skowhegan.
Dean, Edmund, Paris, e Taunton, Mass.
Dearborn, Simon, Monmouth, e Epping, N. H.
Delano, Alpheus, e Friendship, d Friendship March 9, 1826, w Margaret, Friendship.
Delano, Jabez, Livermore, e Winthrop.
Delano, Jonathan, e Duxbery, Mass., d Woolwich September 16, 1833, w Ruth, Woolwich.

Delano, Seth. Phillips, e Winthrop.
Dennison, David, Freeport, e Freeport.
Deshon, James, Waterboro, e Waterboro.
Dickey, Eleazer, Monroe, e Vassalboro.
Didson, Benjamin, Starks, e Dunstable, now Tyngsborough, Mass.
Dingley, Levi, Harpswell. e Duxbury, Mass.
Dix, William, e Dunstable, Mass., d Prospect November 16, 1828, w Abigail, Newburg.
Doane, Amos, Hampden, e Eastham, Mass.
Dodge, Nicholas, e Dunbarton, N. H., d Burnham December 10, 1827, w Elizabeth, Burnham.
Dolbear, Benjamin, Freeman, e Needham, Mass.
Dole, Amos, e Groton, Mass., d Orrington July 20, 1832, w Matilda, Orrington.
Dorman, John, e Kennebunkport, d Kennebunkport July 26, 1828, w Hannah, Kennebunkport.
Doughty, Ichabod, Brunswick, e Kennebec.
Doughty, James, Harpswell, e Brunswick.
Doughty, John, e Freeport, d Portland October 5, 1827, w Dorcas, Freeport.
Doughty, Nathaniel, Portland, e Freeport.
Douglass, John, Denmark, e Scarboro.
Dow, Joseph, e Portland, d Standish October 31, 1805, w Lucy, Standish.
Downing, John, Minot, e Andover, Mass.
Downing, Samuel. Minot, e Andover, Mass.
Doyle, Jonathan, e Harpswell, d Harpswell 1789, w Huldah, Bowdoin.
Dresser, Jonathan, e Fryeburg, d Fryeburg May, 1814, w Elizabeth, Denmark.
Dresser, Richard, Hollis, e Scarboro.
Drown, Stephen, Kennebunkport, e Wells.
Dudley, Nathan. Hebron, e East Sudbury, Mass.
Dunbar, David. Penobscot, e Scituate, Mass.
Dunham, Ammi, Freeport, e Freeport.
Dunham, Moses, Hartford, e Plympton, Mass.
Dunn, Christopher, Belgrade, e Gorham.
Dunn, Joshua, Dixfield, e Durham.
Duron, William, e Edgecomb, d Edgecomb October 21, 1832, w Ruth, Boothbay.
Dwelley, Allen, Springfield, e Pembroke, Mass.

Dyer, Benjamin, Cape Elizabeth, e Cape Elizabeth, d at sea June, 1795, w Hannah, Lisbon.
Dyer, Bickford, e Scarboro, d Baldwin May 5, 1828, w Dolly, Baldwin.
Dyer, Ephraim, e Cape Elizabeth, d Sullivan August 26, 1834, w Hannah, Sullivan.
Dyer, Isaac, Limington, e Cape Elizabeth.

Eastman, Edmund, e Boscawen, N. H., d Limerick December 19, 1812, w Hannah, Limerick.
Eastman, Jacob, Bangor, e Tamworth, N. H.
Eastman, Jacob, Parsonsfield, e Salisbury, Mass.
Eastman, Zachariah, Scarboro, e Cape Ann, Mass.
Eaton, Eliab, Strong, e Reading, Mass.
Eaton, William, Wells, e Wells.
Edmester or Edminster, Noah, Newburg, e Berkley, Mass.
Edwards, Nathaniel, Parsonsfield, e Wells.
Edwards, Thomas (adjutant), e Boston, Mass., d Boston August 4, 1806, w Mary, Portland.
Eldridge, Daniel, e Gorham, d Buxton, June 10, 1832, w Phebe, Turner.
Ellis, Atkins, e Harwich, Mass., d St. Albans October 18, 1833, w Elizabeth, St. Albans.
Ellis, Samuel, e Sandwich, Mass., d East Machias January 27, 1834, w Mary, East Machias.
Emery, David, e Fairfield, d Fairfield November 18, 1830, w Abigail, Fairfield
Emery, Jesse, e Boxford, Mass., d Londonderry, N H., March 27 1812, w Ruth, Newry.
Emery, John, Skowhegan, e Chelmsford, Mass.
Emery, Nathaniel, e Fairfield, d Starks May 1823, w Patence, Anson.
Emery, Samuel, Ripley, e Concord, Mass.
Erskine, Alexander, e Bristol, d Bristol February 20, 1826, w Mary, Bristol.
Erskine, George, Portland, e East Bridgewater, Mass., lost at sea on privateer Dart October, 1812, w Huldah, Portland.
Everton, Zephaniah, Thomaston, e Roxbury, Mass.
Ewer, Jonathan, e Barnstable, Mass., d Vassalboro January 29, 1829, w Betsey, Vassalboro.

Fairfield, John, e Kennebunkport, d Kennebunkport June 10, 1834, w Hannah, Kennebunkport.
Fairfield, William, e Kennebunkport, d Kennebunkport March 14, 1827, w Mary, Kennebunkport.
Fall, George, Lebanon, e Lebanon.
Farnham, Jonathan, e Duxbury, Mass., d Boothbay. May 29, 1822, w Dorcas, Boothbay.
Farrin, John, Bath, e Brunswick.
Farrington, Abner, Warren, e Dedham, Mass.
Fenderson, John, Parsonsfield, e Scarboro.
Fenderson, Peletiah, Scarboro, e Scarboro.
Fickett, Nathaniel, e Cape Elizabeth, d Cape Elizabeth May 3, 1832, w Abigail, Cape Elizabeth.
Fickett, Vinson, Lewiston, e Cape Elizabeth
Field, Daniel, e Buxton, d Hollis June 19, 1798, w Rachel, Greenwood.
Fifield, John, Fryeburg, e Fryeburg
Fillebrown, Thomas, Winthrop, e Massachusetts.
Fish, Adam (captain), e Duxbury, Mass., d Duxbury, Mass, September 26, 1815, w Jane, Bristol.
Fisher, Ebenezer, e Wrentham, Mass., d Brewer March 28, 1835, w Sarah, Brewer.
Fisher, Elijah, Livermore, e Attleboro, Mass.
Fisher, Jacob, Kennebunk, e Wrentham. Mass.
Flagg, Samuel A., Nobleboro, e Boston, Mass.
Fletcher, John, e Acton, Mass., d Sumner March 12, 1835, w Elizabeth, Sumner.
Flood, Henry, e Falmouth, d Buxton October 13, 1834, w Jemima, Buxton.
Flood, James, e Falmouth, w Susanna, Waterboro, m Brown.
Fogg, Charles, Brownfield, e Scarboro.
Fogg, George, Wales, e Scarboro.
Ford, Miles, e Berwick, d Clinton July, 1831, w Susannah, Clinton.
Foss, Elias, Limington, e Scarboro.
Foss, Joseph, Buckfield, e Scarboro.
Foss, Zachariah, Scarboro, e Scarboro.
Foster, Benner, Portland, e Machias.
Foster, Parker, Eliot, e Eliot.
Fowler, Matthew, Unity, e Bridgewater, Mass.
Frank, Thomas, e Falmouth, d Gray October 11, 1831, w Hannah, Gray.

Freeman, Samuel, e Duxbury, Mass., d Minot December 10, 1786, w Hannah, Minot, m Bradford.
Freethy, Joseph, Sedgwick, e Sedgwick.
Freeze, John, e Harpswell, drowned in Penobscot river, w Sarah, Bowdoin, m Card
French, Jacob, e Salisbury. Mass , d Jay April 5, 1819, w Mary, Jay.
Frost, Elliot, Eliot, e Kittery.
Frost, Mark, e Berwick or Lebanon, d Belgrade October 5, 1835, w Hannah, Belgrade.
Frost, Nathaniel, e Kittery, d Eliot February 17, 1829, w Sarah, Eliot.
Frost, Samuel, e Massachusetts, d Wayne October 27, 1823, w Patience, Wayne, m Billington.
Frost, Simon, e Kittery, d Kittery October 1, 1803, w Jane, Cornville, m Morrill.
Frost, Stephen, e Berwick, d Berwick October 8, 1824, w Sarah, Berwick.
Fuller, Andrew, e Middleboro, Mass., d Warren January 31, 1820, w Hannah, Warren.
Fuller, Barzilla, e Kingston, Mass., d Hebron August 8, 1833, w Polly, Hebron.
Fulmer, George, e Bangor, d Sacketts Harbour, N. Y., February 11, 1815, w Nancy, Bangor.
Frye, Nathaniel (paymaster), e Fryeburg, d Fryeburg April 17, 1833, w Dolly, Fryeburg.

Gaitskill, William, e Weymouth, Mass., d Winthrop 1820, w Dorcas, Sidney.
Gammon, Joshua, Cape Elizabeth, e Falmouth.
Gammon, Moses, Oxford, e Gorham
Gardiner, Elijah, Dennysville, e Hingham, Mass.
Gardner, John, Oxford, e Plymouth, Mass.
George, Francis, Leeds, e Taunton, Mass.
George, Thomas, Newport, e Dunbarton, N. H.
Getchell, Zachariah, Wells, e Wells, d at sea autumn of 1792, w Mary, Wells, m Zachariah Goodale.
Gilpatrick, Joseph, Kennebunk, e Wells.
Given, John, Brunswick, e Brunswick.
Glass, Consider, Guilford, e Duxbury, Mass.
Glass, John, Gardiner, e Berwick.
Glidden, Arnold, Chester, e Whitefield.

ALPHABETICAL LIST OF NAMES. 27

Goff, William, e New Gloucester, d in service, w Anna, Sumner, m Tucker.
Goldthwait, Timothy, Augusta, e Stoughton, Mass.
Goodale, Zachariah, e Wells, d Wells September 2, 1825, w Mary, Wells.
Goodwin, George, Avon, e Durham.
Goodwin, Reuben, Lebanon, e Berwick.
Goodwin, Reuben, Jr., e Berwick, d Lebanon February 14, 1827, w Ruth, Lebanon.
Goodwin, Simeon, e Berwick, d Lebanon April 21, 1836, w Mary, Lebanon.
Gordon, Benjamin, Belmont, e Topsham.
Gordon, Caleb, e Pittsfield, Mass., d Augusta July 8, 1833, w Mariam, Augusta.
Gordon, Joseph, Belfast.
Gordon, William, e Andover, Mass., d Fryeburg March 28, 1784, w Bethiah, Portland, m Aaron Chamberlain.
Gove, Jacob, e Saco, d Lubec April 9, 1823, w Martha, Lubec.
Gove, John, e Waterboro, d Limington July 22, 1818, w Lois, Limington.
Gower, John, e Wells, d Wells June 28, 1810, w Mary, Wells.
Grant, Elisha, e Woolwich, d in service August 6, 1777, w Lydia, Wiscasset, m Hilton.
Grant, Joshua, e York, d York June, 1825, w Abigail, York.
Green, Daniel, Readfield, e Durham.
Green, John, e Gorham, d Scarboro October 25, 1809, w Elizabeth, Scarboro.
Green, Jonathan, e Gorham, d Jackson May 26, 1834, w Rebecca, Jackson.
Greenleaf, Enoch, Westport, e Woolwich.
Greenlow, John, Brownfield, e Westbrook.
Griffith, John, e at or near Plympton, Mass., d Livermore February 8, 1840, w Mary, Livermore.
Guilford, John, Hollis, e Scarboro.

Haines, Simeon, Swanville, e New Hampshire.
Hale, Benjamin, Waterford, e Harvard, Mass.
Hale, Israel, Waterford, e Harvard, Mass.
Hall, Charles, Standish, e Standish.
Hall, Enoch, e Windham, d Buckfield December 10, 1835, w Mariam, Buckfield.
Hall, Jabez, Readfield, e Pembroke, Mass.

Hall, John, w Judith, Lyman, m Shackley.
Hall, Levi, Bangor, e Newcastle.
Hall, Luther, e Bowdoinham, w Betsey, Brunswick.
Halloway, William, e Bridgewater. Mass, d Windsor April 16, 1831, w Mary, Windsor.
Ham, John, Monmouth, e Newington, N H.
Ham, Joseph, e Kennebunkport, d Kennebunkport June 3, 1800, w Margaret, Kennebunkport, m Andrew Staples.
Hamblen, Prince, e Gorham, d Gorham April 17, 1836, w Bethiah, Gorham.
Hamilton, Jonathan, Sanford, e Berwick.
Hamilton, Richard, e Berwick, d Searsmont June, 1834, w Mary, Linneus.
Hamilton, William, North Yarmouth. e North Yarmouth.
Hamlin, Africa, e Pembroke, Mass., d Waterford January 20, 1807, w Susanna, Waterford.
Hammond, Paulipus, Peru.
Hancock, William, Buxton, e Buxton.
Hans, James, e Portland, d Portland October 6, 1825, w Hannah, Portland.
Hans, William, e Portland, d Portland September 8, 1830, w Thankful, Portland.
Hanscom, Gideon, late of Lyman, w Mehitable, Kennebunkport.
Hanscom, John, e Kittery, d Litchfield April 27, 1827, w Catherine, Litchfield.
Hanscom, Nathaniel, e Eliot, d Eliot April, 1830, w Lucy, Eliot.
Hanscomb, Reuben, e Kittery, d North Berwick March 2, 1831, w Elice or Alice, North Berwick.
Hardy, William, Wilton, e Windham.
Harlow, Josiah, e Plymouth, Mass., d Waldo August 29, 1825, w Olive, Monroe.
Harmon, Abner, Buxton, e Scarboro.
Harmon, Josiah, Thorndike, e Scarboro.
Harmon, Samuel, Dixmont, e Sanford.
Harmon, Thomas, e Scarboro, d Buxton January 15, 1834, w Mary, Buxton
Harmon, William, Standish, e Scarboro.
Harriman, Simon, e New Hampshire, d Bangor July 29, 1837, w Elizabeth, Bangor.
Harris, John, Litchfield, e Bellingham, Mass.
Hartwell, Oliver, Stetson, e Groton, Mass.

ALPHABETICAL LIST OF NAMES.

Harvest, John Adams, e Waldoboro, d Waldo June 17, 1835, w Anna, Waldo.
Harvey, William, Sou h Berwick, e Kittery.
Haskell, John, e Gorham, d Knox September 22, 1819, w Mary, Knox.
Haskell, Josiah, Thomaston, e Portland.
Haskell, Stephen, e Westbrook, d Levant December 3, 1830, w Rebecca, Topsham.
Haskell, William, e Barnstable, Mass, d China September 15, 1827, w Rhoda, China.
Hatch, Asa, e Gorham, d Gorham December 25, 1798, w Jane, Westbrook.
Hatch, Simeon, e Falmouth, d Dresden October 5, 1802, w Jemima, Dresden.
Hawes, Joseph, Minot, e Needham, Mass
Haynes, Ephraim, Eden, e Harpswell.
Hazen, Jacob, Bridgton, e Boxford, Mass.
Heald, Oliver, Madison, e Westford, Mass.
Heath, William, e N. H., d Mt. Desert September 6, 1840, w Hannah, Mt. Desert.
Heavner, Charles, Waldoboro, e Maine.
Hicks, Samuel, e Falmouth, d Westbrook August 20, 1834, w Clarissa, Portland.
Hill, Daniel, e Biddeford, d Buxton March 10, 1835, w Phebe, Buxton.
Hill, David, e Greenland, N. H, d Waterboro November 27, 1838, w Parnel, Waterboro.
Hill, Thomas, e Falmouth, d North Yarmouth January 5, 1809, w Ruth, Cumberland, m Stubbs.
Hilton, Edward, e Wells, d Wells April 26, 1833, w Mary, Wells.
Hilton, Moral, Wiscasset, e Pownalboro.
Hilton, William, Solon, e Wiscasset.
Hinckley, Seth, e Harwich, Mass., d Eden January 23, 1792, w Genett, Fairfield, m Joseph Mayo.
Hinds, Benjamin, Madison, e Shrewsbury, Mass.
Hinds, Samuel, St. George, e Boston, Mass.
Hine, Richard, e Gorham, d Turner July 26, 1834, w Abiah, Hartford.
Hinkley, Nehemiah, Bluehill, e Brunswick.
Hobbs, Josiah, Falmouth, e Falmouth.

Hodgdon, Jeremiah, e Gorham, d Hebron August 24, 1823, w Thankful. Hebron.
Hodges, Ezra, Hallowell, e Norton, Mass.
Hodgman, John, e Concord, Mass., d Wales February 24, 1834, w Mehitable, Plymouth
Hodsdon, Samuel, e South Berwick, d South Berwick August 2, 1825, w Ann, South Berwick
Hodsdon, Stephen, Rumford, e Berwick.
Hoit, John M., e Portland, d Standish February 6. 1824, w Catherine, Standish.
Holden, Daniel, Sweden, e Stoneham, Mass.
Holden, Samuel, Charleston, e Mendon, Mass.
Holland, Park (lieutenant), Orono, e Petersham, Mass
Hollis, Stephen, e Braintree, Mass, d New Sharon February 7, 1821, w Abigail, New Sharon.
Holmes, Gershom, Minot, e Taunton, Mass.
Holmes, Jonathan, e Plymouth, Mass, d Hartford October 16, 1836, w Mercy, Hartford.
Holt, Darius, Norway, e Andover, Mass.
Holt, John, e Andover, Mass., d Bethel July 16, 1830, w Lydia, Bethel
Holt, William, e Andover, Mass, d Fryeburg May 4, 1827, w Esther, Fryeburg.
Horsom, David, Berwick, e Berwick
Houston, John, Sanford, e Wells.
Houston, Samuel, e Belfast, d Belfast January 9, 1835, w Sarah, Belfast.
Howard, Joseph, Brownfield, e Brownfield.
Howe, Jacob, e Rowley, Mass., d Paris January 30, 1830, w Betsey, Sumner.
Hudson, Timothy, e Winslow, d Clinton April 4, 1834, w Jane, Clinton.
Huff, Daniel, Edgecomb, e Edgecomb.
Huff, Moses, Edgecomb, e Kennebunkport.
Hunnewell, Thomas, e Pownalboro, w Elizabeth, Embden, m Colby.
Hunt, Ichabod, e Gorham, d Unity April 30, 1822, w Eunice, Unity.
Hunton, Jonathan, e Newcastle, d Wiscasset October 16, 1833, w Hannah, Wiscasset.
Huston, John, Sanford, e Wells.

Hutchins, Benjamin, e Westbrook, d Minot September 4, 1810, w Nancy, Minot
Hutchins. Eastman, e Kennebunkport, d Alfred May 8, 1826, w Betsey, Alfred.
Hutchins, Joseph, Hartford, e Falmouth.
Hutchins, Levi, Alfred, e Alfred.
Hutchins, Simeon, Kennebunk, e Kennebunkport.
Hutchins, Thomas, e Waterboro, June 14, 1803, w Abigail, Waterboro.
Hutchinson, Israel, Hallowell, e Lyndeboro, N. H.

Ingalls. Phineas, Bridgton, e Andover, Mass.

Jackman, Richard, Wayne, e Ipswich, Mass.
Jackson, Henry, e Raymond, d Raymond March 23, 1807, w Sarah, Raymond
Jackson, Nathaniel, e Newton, Mass., d Jay November 30, 1830, w Roxanna, Jay.
Jacobs, George (lieutenant), e Wells, d Sanford June 1, 1831, w Hephsibeth, Sanford.
Jacobs, John, Mt Vernon, e Wells.
Jenkins, Lemuel, Bowdoin, e Kittery.
Jenkins, Samuel, e Gorham. d Buckfield November 15, 1832, w Thankful, Buckfield.
Jennings, Eliphalet, Farmington, e Dunstable, Mass.
Jewett, Jonathan, e Rowley, Mass., d Pittston November 19, 1806, w Hannah, Bath, m William S Crooker.
Johnson, Andrew, Stow, e Durham, N. H.
Johnson, Dennis, Waterboro, e Kittery.
Johnson, James, late of Frankfort, e Frankfort, d New York, w Hannah, Augusta.
Johnson, Jasper, d North Yarmouth April 1795, w Rebecca, Pownal, m David Johnson.
Johnson, Nathan, e Deer Isle, d North Yarmouth October 30, 1830, w Mary, Cumberland.
Jones, Joshua, Durham, e Durham.
Jones, Lazarus, Bridgton, e Wells.
Jones, Thomas, e Boston, Mass., d Hope February 6, 1835, w Mary, Hope.
Jordan, Abner, e Limington, d Lisbon September 26, 1819, w Hannah, Auburn.

Jordan, Abraham, e Cape Elizabeth, d Durham April 18, 1835, w Lydia, Durham.
Jordan, David, Albany, e Gray.
Jordan, Hezekiah, e Raymond, d Raymond May 16, 1828, w Eunice, Raymond.
Jordan, Humphrey, e Cape Elizabeth, d Auburn October 13, 1833, w Johannah, Auburn.
Jordan, James, e Windham, d Monroe March 31, 1813, w Hannah, Monroe.
Jordan, Solomon, e Cape Elizabeth, d Cape Elizabeth April 15, 1819, w Sarah, Cape Elizabeth.
Jumper, Daniel, Harrison, e Cape Ann, Mass.

Keen, Isaac, Clinton, e Kittery.
Keezer, David, Calais, e Haverhill, Mass.
Keith, Cornelius, e Bath, d Bath January, 1831, w Lydia, Bath.
Kellock, David, Warren, e Cushing.
Kellogg, Elijah, Portland, e South Hadley, Mass.
Kendall, William, e Clinton, d Fairfield August 11, 1827, w Abigail, Fairfield.
Kenerson, John, e Lebanon, d Denmark October 29, 1833, w Betsey, Denmark.
Kenney, Benjamin, e Wiscasset, d Eastport April, 1815, w Elizabeth, Freedom.
Kenney, Thomas, e Hallowell, d Hallowell April 11, 1825, w Hannah, Pittston.
Kenniston, John, late of Hawke (now Danville), N. H., e Hawke, N. H., d Albany, N. Y., November 28, 1784, w Betsey, Cornville, m Bean.
Keyes, Ebenezer, Jay, e Shrewsbury, Mass.
Kilgore, James, Lovell, e Fryeburg.
Kilgore, John, Newry, e Fryeburg.
Killsa, James, e Bristol, d Thomaston June 25, 1792, w Lydia, Thomaston.
Kimball, David, Harmony, e Wells
Kimball, Joseph, Bridgton, e Waterboro.
Kimball, Nathan, ? Wells, d York October 15, 1827, w Lydia, South Berwick.
Kimball, Rufus, e Scarboro, d Hollis January 27, 1813, w Lucy, Hollis.
King, Moses, e Methuen, Mass., d Hallowell August 10, 1804, w Mary, Pittston, m Brainard.

Kinsley, Daniel, Minot, e Bridgewater, Mass.
Knight, Daniel, Norway, e Gray.
Knight, John, Windham, e Gorham.
Knight, Jonathan, Waterboro, e South Berwick.
Knight, Jonathan, Windham, e Falmouth.
Knight, Joseph, Alfred, e Berwick.
Knight, William, e Nottingham, N. H., d Poland April 11, 1831, w Phebe, Poland.
Knowlton, John, e Ipswich, Mass., d Kittery October 18, 1798, w Dorcas, Eliot.
Knox, Jonathan, Berwick, e Berwick.

Lampson, William, e Edgecomb, d Edgecomb October 15, 1823, w Martha, Edgecomb.
Lancaster, Joseph, Richmond, e Woolwich.
Landerkin, Daniel, Boothbay, e Boothbay.
Lane, John, e Buxton, drowned Whitefield November 1, 1809, w Betsey, Buxton.
Lara, James, Turner, e Falmouth.
Lasdell, Asa, Burnham, e Alfred.
Lassell, Caleb, Waterboro, e Kennebunkport.
Lawrence, John, North Yarmouth, e North Yarmouth.
Leavitt, William, e Exeter, N. H., d Alfred October 22, 1837, w Betsey, Alfred.
Lebroke, James, w Sarah, Greenwood.
Leher, Peter, e Waldoboro, d Washington November 3, 1822, w Catherine, Washington.
Leland, Ebenezer, e Sherburne, Mass., d Deer Isle 1808, w Mary, Brooksville.
Leland, Henry, e Sherburne, Mass , d Sangerville June 26, 1835, w Sarah, Sangerville.
Lemont, Thomas, e Georgetown, d in service October, 1777, w Lucy, Wales, m John Mallett.
Lewis, Abijah, e Buxton, d Hiram December 17, 1830, w Elizabeth, Hiram.
Lewis, Joseph, e York, d Waterboro, December 9, 1834, w Mehitable, Waterboro.
Libby, Allison, e Scarboro, d Gorham May 14, 1816, w Sarah, Limington, m Small.
Libby, Benjamin, e Scarboro, d Whitefield, August 10, 1833, w Hannah, Whitefield.

Libby, Edward, Gorham, e Scarboro.
Libby, Francis, Buxton, e Scarboro.
Libby, Harvey, Limington, e Scarboro.
Libby, James, e Deering, d Auburn May 15, 1828, w Sally, Poland.
Libby, Jonathan (captain), e Scarboro, d Scarboro March 22, 1805, w Abigail, Scarboro.
Libby, Luke, e Scarboro, d in service, w Dolly, Auburn.
Libby, Nathaniel, Limerick, e Kittery.
Libby, Simeon, e Scarboro, d Gorham March 11, 1830, w Ann, Gorham.
Libby, Solomon, e Scarboro, d Saco March 1, 1832, w Sally, Saco.
Libby, Thomas, e Scarboro, d Scarboro March 27, 1827, w Mary, Gorham.
Linscot, Theodore, Sanford, e York.
Littlefield, Abraham, e Wells, d York July 20, 1831, w Susanna, York.
Littlefield, John (ensign), e Wells, d Wells March 11, 1790, w Mariam, Wells.
Littlefield, Moses, Frankfort, e Randolph, Mass.
Lombard, Caleb, e Gorham, d Turner April 19, 1833, w Hannah, Turner.
Lombard, Jedediah, Standish, e Gorham.
Lombard, Nathaniel, Cornville, e Gorham.
Longley, Asa, St. Albans, e Groton, Mass.
Longley, Zachariah, e Groton, Mass., d Dover June 28, 1825, w Betsey, Dover.
Loomis, Roger, e Massachusetts, drowned October 16, 1821, w Isabella, Westport.
Lord, Adam, e Waterboro, d in service 1782, w Olive, Limington, m Stone.
Lord, Daniel, e Berwick, d Limerick December 15, 1833, w Hannah, Limerick.
Lord, Elias, e Berwick, d Lyman February 22, 1833, w Elizabeth, Lyman.
Lord, Nathan, e Berwick, d Lebanon November 26, 1833, w Sarah, Lebanon.
Lord, Richard, e South Berwick, d South Berwick, w Mary, South Berwick.
Lord, Simeon (captain), e Berwick, d South Berwick October 28, 1815, w Polly, North Berwick.

Low, Beniah, of Portland, e Portland, d at sea November 20, 1791, w Elizabeth, Standish, m Lowell.
Low, Jacob, of Bath (captain), e Ipswich, Mass., d in New Jersey in fall of 1803, w Mary, Bath.
Lowell, Benjamin, e Massachusetts, d Bucksport March 10, 1835, w Lydia, Bucksport.
Lowell, Paul, Turner, e Georgetown.
Lowell, Thomas, Dixmont, e Baldwin.
Lunt, Amos, Brunswick, e Falmouth.
Lunt, Daniel (captain), e Westbrook, d Westbrook November 29, 1823, w Eunice, Westbrook.
Lydson, Robey, e Kittery, d Kittery May 27, 1809, w Olive, Kittery.

Madden, John, Waldo, e Cushing.
Maddocks, Samuel, Ellsworth, e Kennebunk.
Margery, Jonathan, e Boston, Mass., d Scarboro November 16, 1820, w Sarah, Scarboro.
Marsh, Noah, e Exeter, N H., d Cornville October 25, 1830, w Hannah, Cornville.
Marston, Nathaniel, born in Newmarket, N. H., d Gardiner September, 1823, w Jane, Gardiner.
Martin, David, Bridgton, e Buxton.
Martin, John, e Scarboro, d Monmouth May 26, 1830, w Lydia, Monmouth.
Martin, Joseph P., Prospect, e Becket, Mass.
Martin, Robert, Sebago, e Saco
Mason, George, e Dresden, d Windsor April 21, 1817, w Susanna, Windsor, m Hilton.
Mason, John, e North Yarmouth, d Falmouth October 22, 1824, w Lucy, Falmouth.
May, John, e New Gloucester, d Raymond December 8, 1813, w Hepsebah, Poland.
Mayberry, William, Raymond, e Windham.
Mayhew, James, Hermon, e Hanson, Mass.
McCausland, Henry, e Gardiner, d Augusta August 12, 1829, w Abiah, Gardiner.
McCausland, James, e Gardiner, d Gardiner March 14, 1826, w Mary, Gardiner.
McClellan, John, Glenburn, e Chester, N. Y.
McDaniel, James, e York, d York August 1821, w Susanna, York.

McDonald, Abner, e Buxton, d Portland, April 29, 1801, w Polly, Windham, m Johnson.
McDonald, Pelatiah, Standish, e Gorham.
McFarland, Elijah, e Plympton, Mass., d Fairfield November 7, 1827, w Sarah, Fairfield.
McFarland, Solomon, e Middleborough, Mass., d Fairfield June 3, 1827, w Deborah, Fairfield, m Scribner.
McGee, Neil, e Bradford, Mass, d Brooksville September 2, 1824, w Susannah, Brooksville.
McGill, William, e Brunswick, d Brunswick September 9, 1828, w Martha, Brunswick.
McIntosh, John, Durham, e Harpswell.
McKenney, Abner, e Scarboro, d Scarboro December 23, 1830, w Sarah, Saco.
McKenney, Joseph, Greene, e Scarboro.
McKenney, William (lieutenant), e Scarboro, d Auburn February 7, 1833, w Mariam, Auburn
McKinney, Jeremy, Saco, e Saco, drowned in Buxton August 14, 1793, w Anna, Saco.
McLucas, John, e Saco, d Hiram March 27, 1813, w Margaret, Waterboro.
McMannus, John, Brunswick, e Brunswick.
McPherson, Dugal, e Boxborough, Mass., d Madison June 11, 1815, w Mary, Madison.
McQuigg, Daniel, e Newcastle, d Newcastle June 5, 1816, w Phebe, Newcastle.
Means, Thomas, e Freeport, d Freeport December 16, 1827, w Eleanor, Freeport.
Mero, Amaziah, Union, e Stoughton, Mass.
Merrick, John, e Weston, Mass., d Skowhegan June 15, 1835, w Mary, Burnham.
Merrill, Daniel (captain), e Kennebunkport, d Kennebunkport September 6, 1808, w Sarah, Kennebunkport.
Merrill, John, Lewiston, e Falmouth.
Merrill, Moses, e Portland, d Portland October 18, 1833, w Elizabeth, Portland.
Merritt, Daniel, e Columbia, d Addison January, 1808, w Hannah, Addison, m William Merritt.
Merritt, William, Addison, e Addison.
Merrow, William, e Biddeford, d Standish March 12, 1836, w Margaret, Standish.

Mighel, Moses, e Exeter, N. H., d Parsonsfield July 23, 1833, w Elizabeth, Parsonsfield.
Miller, Lemuel (lieutenant), Kennebunkport, e Kennebunkport.
Milliken, Joel, Scarboro, e Scarboro.
Milliken, Josiah, e Scarboro, d Limington January 13, 1833, w Sarah, Limington.
Mills, John, e Lebanon, d Belgrade December 21, 1810, w Mary, Belgrade.
Mitchell, John, Harrington, e North Yarmouth.
Mitchell, Joshua, e Bath, d Bath November 1826, w Tamesin, Bath.
Mitchell, Robert, e Cape Elizabeth, d Portland February 3, 1820, w Mary, Portland.
Mitchell, Samuel, Bowdoin, e Wells.
Moody, Daniel, e Scarboro, d Auburn April 23, 1811, w Lucy, Minot.
Moody, George, Limington, e Saco.
Moody, Joshua, e Gorham, d Baldwin December 29, 1829, w Rebecca, Baldwin.
Moore, Joshua, Vienna, e York.
Morrill, Jacob, d Greenbush December 15, 1831, w Olive, Greenbush.
Morrison, Moses, Phippsburg, e Bath.
Morse, Anthony, e Brunswick, w Susa, Brunswick.
Morse, Levi, Gray, e Gray.
Morse, Seth, Paris, e Hopkinton, Mass.
Morton, David, e Gorham, d Gorham June 22, 1827, w Mary, Gorham.
Morton, Thomas, Gorham, e Gorham.
Moulton, Simeon, e Exeter, N. H., d. Newfield April 10, 1834, w Sally, Newfield.
Mugford, John, Windham, e Windham.
Munroe, Hugh, e Rehoboth, Mass., d Thomaston June 22, 1832, w Naomi, Thomaston.
Murch, Matthias, Gorham, e Gorham.

Neal, Samuel, e Kittery, d York December 8, 1816, w Mary, Portsmouth, N. H.
Newbegin, George, Parsonsfield, e Scarboro.
Nichols, Bela, e Cohasset, Mass., d Prospect November 18, 1831, w Dorcas, Prospect.

Nichols, Nathaniel, e Rehoboth, Mass., d Augusta May 28, 1836, w Mehitable, Augusta.
Nickerson, Reuben, e Eastham, Mass., d Frankfort August 17, 1831, w Lois, Frankfort.
Norman, John, late of Kennebunk, e Wells, w Sally, Kennebunk.
Norton, Nathaniel, e Sanford, d Limington November 22, 1831, w Hannah, Limington.
Nowell, Zachariah, Portland, e Portland.
Noyes, Bela, e Bridgewater, Mass , d Norway August 24, 1833, w Elizabeth, Greenwood.
Nutting, Abel, e Groton, Mass., d Lisbon January 18, 1827, w Rhoda, Lisbon, m Green.
Nutting, Thomas, Wilton, e Littleton, Mass.
Nye, Jonathan, Fairfield, e Sandwich, Mass.

Oakes, John, Exeter, e Canaan.
O'Brien, John, Cornish, e Kittery.
Orr, Alexander (lieutenant), e Boston, Mass., left Boston 1783 never heard from, w Deborah, Camden, m Ames.
Osborn, Hugh, Rome, e Pembroke, Mass.
Osborn, James, Kennebunk, e Woburn, Mass.
Osborn, Michael, e Pembroke, Mass., d Wiscasset December 4, 1834, w Judith, Augusta.
Osgood, Asa, e Andover, Mass., d Hiram August 10, 1833, w Hannah, Hiram.
Owen, Philip, Brunswick, e Topsham.

Packard, James, Norway, e Bridgewater, Mass.
Packard, Nehemiah, Minot, e Bridgewater, Mass.
Page, Abraham, born Kensington, N. H., w Dorothy, Belgrade.
Page, Chase, e Deerfield, N. H., d Corinth May 4, 1825, w Lydia, Levant.
Page, Daniel, Fairfield, e Haverhill, Mass.
Paine, Thomas, Pownal, e Portland.
Palmer, Simon, Windsor, e Warner, N. H.
Parker, Edmund, e Pepperell, Mass., d Norridgewock, son and heir, Edmund, Norridgewock.
Parker, John, e Westbrook, d Westbrook 1788, w Anne, Westbrook.
Parker, Josiah, New Portland, e Fairfield.
Parkhurst, Nathan, e New Hampshire, d Unity May 17, 1815, w Sarah, Unity.

ALPHABETICAL LIST OF NAMES. 39

Parsons, Nathan (adjutant), e Massachusetts, d Bangor October 11. 1822, w Susan, Bangor.
Partridge, David, e Falmouth, d Poland March 22, 1834, w Mary, Poland.
Patch, George, e Kittery, d Kittery February 17, 1816, w Sally or Sarah, Kittery.
Patten, Nathaniel, Penobscot, e Westminster, Mass.
Patterson, James, e Saco, d Hollis April 1, 1816, w Lucretia, Saco.
Paul, David, Lewiston, e New Gloucester.
Payne, William, Anson, e Woolwich.
Peary, Stephen, Denmark, e Wells.
Peck, Joshua, e Rehoboth, Mass., d Clinton April 16, 1833, w Diadema S., Clinton.
Pendexter, Paul, Cornish, e Biddeford.
Penney, Abraham, Smithfield, e Wells.
Penney, George, e Wells, d Belgrade March 27, 1814, w Abigail, Wells.
Penney, Salathiel, Waterville, e Wells.
Perkins, Samuel, e Newton, Mass., d Paris January 8, 1809, w Mehitable, Paris.
Perry, Jesse, e Rehoboth, Mass , d Steuben December 18, 1832, w Mary, Steuben.
Pettee, Oliver, e Walpole, Mass., d Gouldsboro August 3, 1831, w Abigail, Gouldsboro.
Philbrook, David, e Hallowell, d Hallowell, February 17, 1831, w Catherine, Hallowell
Phillips, Ichabod, e Turner, d Leeds October 13, 1830, w Elizabeth, Canton, m Ames.
Phillips, Jairus, e Pembroke, Mass., d Turner June 3, 1828, w Silence, Turner.
Phinney, John, Gorham, e Gorham.
Picket, William, New Gloucester, e New Gloucester.
Pillsbury, Nathan, e Kittery, d Thomaston May 23, 1826, w Lucy, Thomaston.
Plaisted, John, e Scarboro, d Standish January 26, 1834, w Lydia, Standish.
Plummer, Edward, Albion, e Scarboro.
Plummer, Isaac, e Scarboro, d Gorham July 12, 1821, w Esther, Gorham.
Plummer, John, Freedom, e Scarboro.
Plummer, William, Auburn, e Scarboro.

Poland, Joseph, e Beverly, Mass., d in service at Washington, D. C., 1813, w Hannah, Cumberland.
Pollard, Barton, e Raymond, N. H., d Albion September 10, 1828, w Mary, Albion.
Poole, Job, Falmouth, e Falmouth.
Poole, Thomas, e Falmouth, d Brunswick April 19, 1824, w Rebecca, Brunswick.
Porter, Benjamin J. (surgeon's mate), Camden, had lived in Topsham.
Pratt, Elam, e Abington, Mass., d Skowhegan April 18, 1836, w Lydia, Skowhegan.
Pratt, George, Salem, e Middleborough, Mass.
Proctor, Samuel, e Falmouth, d Durham March 12, 1795, w Joanna, Wayne, m Thompson
Pullen, John, e Attleboro, Mass., d Waterville March 29, 1810, w Amy, Waterville.
Pullen, Oliver, Palermo, e Attleboro, Mass.
Pumpilly, Bennett, e Pembroke, Mass., d Turner December 5, 1834, w Elizabeth, Turner.

Ramsdell, James, e Lynn, Mass., d Lubec June 2, 1829, w Juda, Lubec, m Robinson.
Randall, James, e Berwick, d Limington May 15, 1821, w Mary, Limington.
Randall, Stephen, e Berwick, d Limerick September 18, 1837, w Elizabeth, Limerick.
Rankins, James, e Lebanon, d Rome November 22, 1799, w Sarah, Lebanon.
Redington, Asa, Waterville, e Wilton, N. H.
Reed, Amaziah, e North Yarmouth, d Weld March 18, 1833, w Jediah, Weld.
Reed, Ward, Dixmont, e Woburn, Mass.
Reynolds, Daniel, e Middleborough, Mass., d Burnham May 13, 1832, w Thankful, Burnham.
Reynolds, David, d Dennysville March 31, 1832, w Rebecca, Dennysville.
Reynolds, Eliphalet, Addison, e New London, Conn.
Rhode Island, Newport, e Newbury, Mass , w Phillis, Deer Isle.
Rhodes, Jacob, Lyman, e Kennebunkport.
Rhodes, Moses, Waterboro, e Kennebunkport.
Riant, Joseph, Farmington, e Thornton, N. H.
Richards, Joseph, Saco, e Scarboro.

ALPHABETICAL LIST OF NAMES. 41

Richardson, Joel, e Topsham, d Durham February 20, 1827, w Lydia, Guilford.
Ricker, Simeon, Lisbon, e Berwick.
Rideout, Abraham, Kennebunkport, e Brunswick.
Rideout, William, e Falmouth, d Cumberland January 23, 1831, w Ruth, Cumberland.
Ridley, David, Windsor, e Gorham.
Ridley, George, e. Harpswell, d Bowdoin October 31, 1818, w Mary, Bowdoin, m Rogers.
Roach, John, e "Little Winzor," N. H., d Wilton August 22, 1828, w Abigail, Wilton.
Robbins, Daniel, Leeds, e Augusta.
Robbins, Eliphalet, Norridgewock, e Douglas, Mass.
Robbins, Otis, Thomaston, e Thomaston.
Robinson, George, e Cape Elizabeth, d Hollis March, 1819, w Isabella, Hollis.
Robinson, John, e Scarboro, d Limington February 14, 1826, w Deborah, Limington.
Robinson, John, e Watertown, Mass., d Sebago February 20, 1827, w Phebe, Sebago.
Robinson, Samuel, late of Portland, e Cape Elizabeth, d at sea August 21, 1806, w Betsey, Portland.
Robinson, William, e York, d in service 1782, w Sarah, York.
Rogers, John, St. Albans.
Rolf, Jeremiah, Abbot, e Buxton.
Rollins, Eliphalet, Hallowell, e Newcastle.
Rollins, John, Augusta, e Newcastle.
Rose, Benjamin, Hartland, e Bangor.
Rourke, Martin, e Massachusetts, d Durham June 1, 1807, w Elizabeth, Durham.
Rowe, Webber, Baldwin, e Standish.
Rumery, Dominicus, e Kittery, d Lubec October 27, 1835, w Pamelia, Lubec.
Runnells, John, e Scarboro, d Saco July 7, 1816, w Rhoda, Portland.
Runnells, Thomas, Portland, e Queenstown, Md.
Russell, Andrew. Madison, e Townsend, Mass.
Russell, Calvin, Moscow, e Groton, Mass.

42   SOLDIERS OF THE AMERICAN REVOLUTION.

Sanborn, Simeon, e Standish, d Bethel October 28, 1832, w Hannah, Greenwood.
Sanders, Joseph, e Wareham, Mass., d Farmington September 12, 1831, w Lucy, Farmington.
Sanford, John, Cape Elizabeth. e Cape Elizabeth.
Sargent, Charles, South Berwick, e York temporarily in Portsmouth, N. H.
Sargent, John, e York, d Frankfort November 23, 1801, w Lydia, Frankfort.
Sargent, Paul Dudley (colonel), e Amherst, N. H., d Sullivan September 15, 1827, w Lucy, Sullivan.
Sawyer, Josiah, Steuben, e Cape Elizabeth.
Seavey, Eliakim, York, e York.
Severance, Caleb, Brewer, e Newburyport, Mass.
Severance, Ephraim, e Kingston, N. H., d Belmont March 6, 1826, w Ruth, Knox.
Sewall, Henry (captain), Augusta, e York.
Shackley, Joseph, Lyman, e Wells
Shane, Richard, e Berwick, d Raymond March 31, 1828, w Susannah, Raymond.
Shaw, Abraham, York, e York.
Shaw, Ephraim, e Middleborough, Mass , d Sidney January 27, 1835, w Rebecca, New Vineyard.
Shaw, John, Woolwich, e Woolwich.
Shaw, Nathaniel, e Portland, d Portland August 16, 1831, w Polly, Portland.
Shaw, Nathaniel, Turner, e Abington, Mass.
Shed, Amos, e Groton, Mass., d Norridgewock July 11, 1800, w Lucy, Norridgewock, m Crosby.
Shed, Lemuel, e Leominster, Mass , d Norway June 1818, w Ruth, Norway.
Sheldon, William, e Woolwich, d Newcastle December 26, 1831. w Sarah, Newcastle.
Shepherd, James, e Jefferson, d Jefferson July 24, 1818, w Mary, Jefferson.
Shepherd, Lewis, e Scarboio, d Portland November 20, 1832, w Elizabeth, Portland.
Shepherd, William, e Jefferson, d Jefferson March 17, 1832, w Lucy, Jefferson.
Sherman, James, e Freeport, d Freeport 1789, w Margaret, Freeport.

Silley, Benjamin, Brooks, e Gorham
Simmons, Joel, e New Gloucester, d Harrison February 24, 1815, w Artemisa, Minot, m Packard.
Simonton, Walter, e Cape Elizabeth, d Cape Elizabeth May 28, 1826, w Lucy, Cape Elizabeth.
Simpson, Simeon, Winslow, e Winslow.
Sinclair, Joseph, Bangor, e Barnstead, N. H.
Skinner, John, Lewiston, e Cape Elizabeth.
Skriggins, Thomas, Eliot, e Eliot.
Small, Daniel, Limington, e Scarboro.
Small, Daniel, Raymond, e Cape Elizabeth.
Small, Henry, e Scarboro, d Limington November 9, 1826, w Elizabeth, Limington.
Small, James, Scarboro, e Scarboro.
Small, Jeremiah, Westbrook, e Windham.
Smith, Charles, Belfast, e Woolwich.
Smith, Ebenezer (captain), e Woolwich, d Woolwich September, 24, 1824, w Jennet, Richmond.
Smith, Jesse, e Milton, Mass., d Bangor November 21, 1829, w Lucy, Bangor.
Smith, John, e Gloucester, Mass., d Islesboro May 15, 1824, w Lydia, Belfast, m Covel.
Smith, John 4th, e Boston, Mass., d Mt. Desert June 7, 1828, w Anna, Mt. Desert.
Smith, John Kilby (captain), Portland, e Boston, Mass.
Smith, Moses, Prospect, e Sturbridge, Mass.
Smith, Noah, e Biddeford, d Hollis October 15, 1830, w Comfort, Hollis.
Smith, Peleg, e Woolwich, d Hope June 12, 1832, w Lucy Ann, Hope.
Smith, Roland, Augusta, e Middleborough, Mass.
Smith, Samuel, Monroe, e Buxton.
Smith, Stephen, Freedom, e Bristol.
Smith, Thomas, Litchfield, e Georgetown.
Snow, Paul M., late of Portland, e Wells, d at sea October 23, 1815, w Mary, Saco.
Soule, Asa, Montville, e Halifax, Mass.
Southard, Constant, e Duxbury, Mass., d Corinna November 19, 1826, w Lucy B., Corinna.
Spaulding, Samuel, Frankfort, e Chelmsford, Mass.
Spearing, John, e Clinton, d Hartland November 9, 1831, w Mary, Frankfort.

Spencer, Solomon, Hartland, e Winslow.
Spencer, Thomas, Limington, e Berwick.
Spencer, William, e South Berwick, d Baldwin May 29, 1835, w Eleanor, Baldwin.
Spring, Josiah, Brownfield, e Brownfield.
Spurr, Enoch, Otisfield, e Wrentham, Mass.
Stanford, John, Bath, e Ipswich, Mass.
Stanley, Adin, Winthrop, e Attleborough, Mass.
Staples, Joseph, e Biddeford, d Biddeford January 21, 1832, w Louisa, Biddeford.
Staples, Stephen, e Topsham, d Lisbon May 18, 1814, w Charity, Lisbon.
Staples, William, e Sanford, d Bethel February 15, 1832, w Joan, Bethel.
Starbird, Samuel, Lisbon, e Brunswick.
Stetson, Hezekiah, e Plympton, Mass., d Sumner March 3, 1833, w Chloe, Hartford.
Stevens, Daniel, e Thomaston, d Thomaston April, 1796, w Jerusha, Hallowell, m Davenport.
Stevens, Jonas, e Gray, d Norway February 9, 1833, w Mary, Norway.
Stevens, Samuel, e Townsend, Mass , d Mercer September 14, 1833, w Amy, Mercer.
Stevens, Thomas, Brooksville, e Groton, Mass.
Steward, Amasa, Skowhegan, e Lunenburg, Mass.
Steward, Benjamin, e Lunenburg, Mass., d Skowhegan February 7, 1820, w Sally, Newport.
Stinson, Samuel, Deer Isle, e Deer Isle.
Stinson, William, e Woolwich, d Richmond March 9, 1823, w Abiah, Litchfield.
Stoddard, Nathaniel, e Hingham, Mass., d Perry October 20, 1828, w Hannah, Perry.
Stone, George, Limington, e Scarboro.
Stone, John, Parsonsfield, e Scarboro.
Stone, Jonathan, e Cape Elizabeth, d Gorham, April 19, 1834, w Damaris, Gorham.
Storer, Ebenezer (paymaster), Gorham, e Wells.
Storer, Joseph, e Westbrook, d in service October, 1777, w Joanna, Portland.
Storer, William, e Maine, d Hiram, April 13, 1826, w Sarah, Hiram.

Stover, Christopher, e Harpswell, d Appleton September 8, 1828, w Catherine, Appleton.
Strout, Isaac, e Cape Elizabeth, d Limington, March 3, 1818, w Mary, Limington.
Sturtevant, Asa, Dover, e Middleborough, Mass.
Sturtevant, Francis, e Plympton, Mass , d Paris May 6, 1833, w Mary, Paris.
Sturtevant, Joseph, e Wareham, Mass., d Hebron March 20, 1835, w Sarah, Paris.
Sturtevant, Lot, Waterville, e Wareham, Mass.
Sturtevant, Seth, Sumner, e Halifax, Mass.
Sutton, John, e York, d Limington November 18, 1819, w Lois, Limington.
Swett, Israel, Cape Elizabeth, e Falmouth.
Swett, John, Windham, e Windham.
Swett, Joshua, Gorham, e Portland.

Tappan, Michael, born in Manchester, Mass , d Gardiner August 5, 1831, w Hannah, Gardiner.
Tarbell, Joseph, e Pepperell, Mass., d Norridgewock August 20, 1826, w Mariam, Norridgewock.
Taylor, Ephraim, Newcastle, e Newcastle.
Taylor Noah, Sanford, e Wells.
Thayer, Peter, e Plympton, Mass., d Hebron February 2, 1788, w Ruth, Oxford.
Thomes, W. (See Introduction. page 10.)
Thompson, Alexander, e Kennebunkport, d Topsham February 23, 1820, w Lydia, Topsham.
Thompson, Benjamin (lieutenant), e Brunswick, d Topsham February 9, 1793, w Rhoda, Topsham, m Isaac Johnson.
Thompson, Ephraim, Lyman, e Kennebunkport.
Thompson, James, e Derryfield, N. H., d at sea October 19, 1805, w Hannah, Calais.
Thompson, James, Kennebunkport, e Kennebunkport.
Thompson, Joseph, e Falmouth, d Lewiston May 26, 1827, w Happy, Bangor.
Thompson, Joseph, York, e York.
Thompson, Richard, e Brunswick, d Wales September 23, 1831, w Bathsheba, Wales.
Thompson, William, e Falmouth, d Wayne November 28, 1833, w Joanna, Wayne.

Thurston, Jacob, e Wrentham, Mass., d Otisfield 1821, w Ann B., Otisfield, m John Piper.
Tibbetts, Giles, e Boothbay, d Boothbay July 9, 1832, w Susan, Boothbay.
Tibbetts, Stephen, Bristol, e Bristol
Tobin, Samuel, e Windham, d Buckfield December 29, 1834, w Margaret, Buckfield.
Toby, John, e Portland, d Portland November 12, 1834, w Margaret, Portland.
Toothaker, Seth, Harpswell, e Harpswell.
Tourtelott, Abraham, e Massachusetts, d Orono December 7, 1820, w Leah, Howland.
Town, Joseph, Kennebunk, e Bowdoin.
Townsend, Daniel, e Vassalboro, d in service 1778, w Sarah, Sidney, m Sawtelle.
Tripp, Robert, Sanford, e Sanford.
True, Obediah, Denmark, e Sanford.
True, Zebulon, e North Yarmouth, d Temple February 4, 1830, w Martha, Temple.
Turner, David, New Vineyard, e Middleborough, Mass.
Turner, Isaac, Durham, e North Yarmouth.
Turner, Robert, e Bristol, d Belmont November 29, 1836, w Elizabeth, Belmont.
Turner, Starbird, Rome, e Freeport
Tuttle, Samuel (lieutenant), Portland, e Lynn, Mass.
Tyler, Abraham, Saco, e Scarboro.
Tyler, Andrew, Frankfort, e Scarboro.
Tyler, Daniel, Brownfield, e Haverhill, Mass.

Ulmer, George, Hope, e Waldoboro.
Uran, James, e Saco, d Waterboro February 11, 1824, w Anna, Waterboro.

Varrel, Samuel, Minot, e Gloucester, Mass.
Vance, William, Readfield, e Boston, Mass.
Vining, John, e Durham, d Durham October 27, 1837, w Mary, Durham.

Wagg, James, Durham, e Cape Elizabeth.
Waistcoat, Joshua, e Cape Elizabeth, d Buckfield February 6, 1826, w Deborah, Hartford.
Wakefield, Gibbons, e Kennebunk, d Westbrook March 14, 1807, w Nancy, Westbrook.

Walker, Edward, e Berwick, d Waterboro November 5, 1832, w Susan, Waterboro.
Walker, John, e Woolwich, d Anson March 22, 1831, w Nancy, Anson.
Walker, John, e Hopkinton, Mass., d Livermore May 7, 1809, w Mary, Livermore.
Walton, Benjamin, Chester, e Brunswick.
Warden, Thomas, e Marblehead, Mass., d Wells February 15, 1827, w Ednar, Wells.
Wardwell, Joseph, Rumford, e Andover, Mass
Warren, Abijah, Paris, e Worcester, Mass.
Warren, Daniel, Limerick, e Hollis.
Warren, Nathaniel, e Scarboro, d Hiram August 4, 1819, w Margaret, Hiram.
Warren, Pelatiah, Monmouth, e Durham.
Wasgatt, Davis, Mt. Desert, e Monson. Mass.
Wasson, John, Brooksville, e Shirley, Mass
Wasson, Thomas, Brooksville, e Shirley, Mass.
Waterhouse, Joseph, Standish, e Scarboro.
Waterman, Joseph, Knox, e Halifax, Mass.
Waterman, Malachi, e Gorham, d Baldwin February 12, 1824, w Mary, Baldwin.
Watson, John, e Taunton, Mass., d Bowdoinham May 2, 1823, w Eunice, Richmond.
Webb, Edward, Gorham, e Windham.
Webb, Nathaniel, e Woolwich, d Newcastle December 25, 1832, w Lydia, Newcastle.
Webber, George, Richmond, e Kennebunk.
Webber, John, e Wells, d Industry, October 13, 1808, w Eunice, Litchfield, m Stevens.
Webber, Jonathan, Kennebunk, e Wells.
Webber, Joseph, e Cape Elizabeth, d at sea March 1, 1785, w Elizabeth, Portland, m Woodbury.
Welch, James, Gray, e York.
Welch, Lemuel, Durham, e Durham.
Welch, Paul e York, d York, w Mary, York.
Weld, Benjamin (commissary in the hospital department), Brunswick, e Boston, Mass.
Wells, James, e Raymond, N. H., d Vienna December 11, 1818, w Mary, Rome.

Wentworth, John, e Ellsworth, d Belmont September 27, 1827, w
  Lydia, Ellsworth.
Wentworth, Lemuel, Hope, e Stoughton, Mass.
Wentworth, Paul, of Knox, e Berwick, d on a visit in Prospect
  September 4, 1833, w Mary, Knox.
Wescott, Isaac, Gorham, e Scarboro.
Wescott, Samuel, e Cape Elizabeth, d Cape Elizabeth November
  15, 1799, w Nancy, Portland.
West, Isaac, Jay, e Bridgewater or Newton, Mass.
Weston, Joseph, Otisfield, e Gorham.
Whidden, James, born in Penobscot, d Canaan March 29, 1828, w
  Sally, Canaan.
Whidden, Solomon, Skowhegan, e Dresden.
White, Joshua, e Leominster, Mass., d Fairfield April 21, 1828, w
  Margaret, Fairfield.
Whiting, Sampson, Denmark, e Andover, Mass.
Whitney, Isaac, Lisbon, e Georgetown.
Whitney, Jesse, e Gorham, d Saco January 17, 1831, w Charity,
  Saco.
Whitten, John, e Topsham, d Topsham November 1, 1826, w Jane,
  Topsham.
Whitten, Richard, Troy, e Scarboro.
Wilcox, John, Monmouth, e Tiverton, R. I.
Wiley, Ephraim, St. George, e St. George.
Wilkins, Edward, late of Charleston, e East Sudbury, Mass., d
  from home in Enfield March 9, 1831, w Bridget, Exeter.
Williams, John, Wiscasset, e Taunton, Mass.
Williams, Lemuel (lieutenant), e Woolwich, d Anson September
  22, 1820, w Anna, Anson.
Willis, James, e Bridgewater, Mass., d Minot July 18, 1830, w
  Sally, Minot.
Willis, Thomas, e Topsfield, Mass., d St. George January 9, 1795,
  w Joanna, St. George.
Wills, James, Belgrade, e Boston, Mass.
Wilson, Charles, e Raymond, d in service 1778, w Achsah, Ray-
  mond, m Jordan.
Wilson, Edward, Cumberland, e Gorham.
Wilson, Mark, e Falmouth, d Jay August 23, 1804, w Olive, Canton.
Wilson, Samuel, e Conway, N. H., d Conway December 10, 1787,
  w Ruth, Orono, m Samuel Sterling.
Wing, Nathan, e Gorham, d Abbot April 10, 1836, w Love, Abbot.

Winn, Samuel (lieutenant), e Wells, d Wells January 28, 1818, w Lois, Kennebunk.
Winslow, Abraham, e Freeport, d Freeport February 6, 1806, w Elizabeth, Freeport.
Winslow, Ezekiel, e Newcastle, d Waldoboro June 13, 1835, w Sedonah, Waldoboro.
Winslow, John, e Petersham, Mass., d Minot July 14, 1834, w Mary, Minot.
Winter, Joseph, e Newburyport, Mass , d Carthage June 13, 1832, w Betsy, Jay, m Morse.
Witham, Caleb, e Georgetown, d Woolwich August 5, 1823, w Lucretia, Woolwich.
Witham, James, e Kittery, d Kittery December 2, 1833, w Olive, Kittery.
Witham, Jedediah, e Kittery, killed at Monmouth battle June 28, 1778, w Hannah, Eliot, m John Tuttle, then m Timothy Spinney.
Withee, Uzziel, Hartland, e Massachusetts.
Withee, Zoe, Industry, e Haverhill, Mass.
Withington, Robert, e Wrentham, Mass , d Monmouth August 19, 1823, w Abigail, Monmouth, daughter and only heir, Sarah Richardson.
Wood, Jesse (alias Atwood), Wilton, e Monson, Mass.
Wood, Josiah, Porter, e Dracut, Mass
Wood, Thomas, e Middleborough, Mass., d Hebron September 28, 1824, w Lois, Hebron.
Woodbridge, Christopher (captain), e Newcastle, d Newcastle May 19, 1825, w Sarah, Hallowell.
Woodman, Ephraim, e Buxton, d Buxton March 23, 1828, w Elizabeth, Buxton.
Woodward, James, e Bridgewater, Mass., d Bowdoinham February 12, 1830, w Ruth, Bowdoinham.
Worster, Thomas, e Berwick, d Sanford March, 1822, w Susan, Sanford.
Wright, John, Bluehill, e Andover, Mass.
Wright, Joseph, Raymond, e Wrentham, Mass.
Wyman. Henry, Madison, e Petersham, Mass.
Wyman, Reuben, Fairfield, e Worcester, Mass.

Yeulin, William, Skowhegan, e New Gloucester.
Young, Abraham, e Gray, d Gray January, 1829, w Rebecca,
   Paris, m Washburn.
Young, James, e Woolwich or Wiscasset, d at sea 1796, w Abigail,
   Readfield, m Elliot.
Young, John, e York, d York 1798, w Hannah, York.
Young, Joseph, e Wells, w Martha, Kennebunk.
Young, Nathaniel, Greenwood, e Gray.

www.ingramcontent.com/pod-product-compliance
Lightning Source LLC
Chambersburg PA
CBHW071751090426
42738CB00011B/2645